# TalOp Client Relationship Management

WILLIAM A. HOWATT
TYLER HAYDEN
CONSTANCE ROBINSON

**Howatt HR Consulting Inc.**

ISBN 978-0-9920571-0-7

Published 2013

Howatt HR Consulting Inc.
6585 Hwy. 221
Kentville NS B4N 3V7

# Preface

The core of this book is the work of Bill Howatt and Tyler Hayden. Given my love of writing and my own experience as a student of client service, I was invited to offer some thoughts and comments before it went to print.

As I prepared my notes, I found the analogy of an apple tree frequently coming to mind. A successful and sustainable organization is like a healthy apple tree. The farmer knows that so long as the tree is healthy, it will bear apples of a particular type and size, sweetness, and colour.

The species of the tree is the brand that carries a particular expectation of the fruit it will bear. If the tree fails to bear the apple promised, the farmer will be disappointed, confused, and unlikely to invest in the care of that tree. This is like the expectation of clients of an organization. Through the organization's brand, clients expect a product that will be available in a particular time frame (early summer or late fall), appearance, quality (firm or sweet), and utility.

The analogy applies to the authors' model for client relations management (the H&H CRM Model described in chapter 1). While an apple tree may appear to be healthy on the outside, there may be concerns of an infestation that threatens its health from the inside. For a season or two, the tree may manage to bear fruit that meets the quality standards the farmer expects. However, if the internal health of the tree is not attended to, its success will not be sustainable.

Similarly, an organization that ignores its internal health may be able to supply clients with the quality product they expect for a time. However, the sustainability of that standard is at serious risk if employees don't take pride in their organization, don't care about whether the product or service meets client expectations, and have disengaged. Therefore, the H&H CRM Model requires organizations to build customer service from the inside out.

The apple tree analogy is also helpful in explaining why the H&H CRM Model is not simply a boiler plate template for the reader to fill in the blanks and declare that they have a client relationship management (CRM) model. A CRM model should not be a component that is added onto an organization like a branch grafted onto a tree. The brand of the tree promises one type of apple; grafting from another tree will result in a fruit that does not satisfy the brand expectation.

An organization's CRM model has to be generated from its roots and all of its components, if the result is to be aligned with the anticipated product or service. The authors provide a practical and neat model for client relations management, grounded in solid theory and offering straightforward tools for action.

This book was written to help those managers and leaders who recognize the need for a CRM model but are uncertain of where to start. It is our belief that this framework will help the dreams you have for your organization to bear wonderful fruit.

— *Constance Robinson*

# Contents

# Introduction

The prime objective of client relationship management (CRM) is to protect a company's most important asset: its established client base. The goal is to build and add clients as well as retain loyal clients who trust the organization's product or service.

It can take up to two years of building trust to establish the relationship needed to close high value deals; if one client is turned off during that time, they can spread the bad news to others. Research shows that one bad experience can result in the loss of up to 12 clients.

Despite the importance of client relations, even in service-based organizations, a structured approach to client relations remains a significant gap for many. A service-based culture provides benefits across the whole organization and supports its success. Human resources professionals and managers prove their strategic value to CEOs by optimizing both internal and external clients' experiences; taking steps to enhance CRM is a high-impact means of delivering on this.

Client relationship management is really straight forward; clients want and need two things: to be respected, and to believe that they are valued (Fox). However, ensuring that these two objectives are achieved with each and every client is where things can start to get a bit complicated. This is especially so in large and complex organizations where there may be many different interpretations of what is required to show respect and deliver value. Creating a shore division and understanding of the organization's client service standards is key. Integrating a well-thought-out client service plan takes time. An industry-accepted benchmark for a mid-size company (500-1,500 employees) is that it takes about two years to design and fully implement a CRM plan. While design and implementation may take time, the impact of a CRM model is soon felt. The outcome of a well-thought-out plan can be noticed within 6 to 12 months.

Building a strong approach to client relationship management requires a logical, seamless, and timely response to clients. Many organizations spend considerable effort reaching out to their "buying" clients without also investing in their internal clients — their employees. Without attending to a service-based culture, the sustainability of CRM initiatives is at risk; the employees are the torch bearers for the CRM plan. If they don't embrace the value of CRM, any CRM initiative will wither as just a flash-in-the plan program.

The risk of unseen erosion of the service culture accelerates as more people leave or retire from an organization. It is essential that the people that inherit the brand of an organization understand the role of the client experience in defining that brand. Buying into the corporate culture is as important to brand preservation and organizational success as selling. Companies that provide their employees with a strong client service approach will reap the benefits of a dedicated and engaged workforce that can deliver the promised client experience.

Client relationship management encompasses the methodology and techniques that inspire trust (both internally and externally) in client service promises. The goal of this book is to introduce key issues to consider when teaching and promoting CRM. It offers insights into how to think about clients and their needs.

As a follow-up to *TalOp: Taking the Guesswork Out of Management,* this book applies the TalOp® methodology to client relationship management. It explains how CRM must be embedded in all facets of an organization so that customer relations is not merely a veneer that is applied by the sales team; instead, a CRM model must be a reflection of the core values of the entire organization.

This book will enhance a leader's understanding of how to begin or continue to build on the great things already being done to engage with clients. Developing a CRM program must start with a methodology that can provide a framework for ensuring that the organization is keeping the client focus in all its aspects.

Chapter 1 offers the TalOp methodology and the H&H CRM Model for clearly defining the roles and expectations that must be met in order to deliver quality service and nurture client relations. It introduces the role of client caretakers.

Chapter 2 applies the ABCs of CRM as expressed in the H&H CRM Model.

Chapter 3 offers some additional insights into CRM for those who have direct contact with clients.

Chapter 4 outlines steps to establishing client confidence.

The Appendix is a toolbox of lists and worksheets that managers can choose from to keep client relations front-of-mind for every client and for every day.

# CHAPTER 1

# CRM Theory

Organizations that use client relationship management recognize that their success is defined by client satisfaction. Translating this recognition into results requires a defined strategy and plan for increasing the likelihood that clients will have a positive experience. The client experience will be influenced by an organization's CRM approach.

CRM is not just about promoting the obvious: smiling and being interactive and polite to clients. An effective CRM model does much more. It outlines how an organization can consistently facilitate the client experience. The CRM model's level of detail depends on the organization's expectations of those who are assigned to interact with clients.

A small business with one owner/employee and one product offering may not require much detail because of the simplicity of the organization. However, as more people are added and as more offerings are made available to clients, the potential grows for client expectations to be missed.

A great sales person can only do so much if the product does not match up with client expectations, or the repair and servicing department is lousy. A quality CRM model impacts more than the sales team. It must penetrate all levels of the organization. If the senior leadership does not value CRM and measures only the most recent profit statement, client relations will suffer over time as this perspective percolates through the workforce. Therefore, the CRM approach must permeate all aspects of the organization, from the most senior of decision makers through to those who clean the offices and the windows. Everyone in the organization contributes to the client experience.

## The TalOp Methodology

The TalOp methodology embraces a pan-organization approach for CRM. Dr. William Howatt is an industrial/organizational psychologist who works with organizations at the strategic level and helps leaders ensure the alignment of their customer service philosophy with their strategic objectives. Early in his consulting work, Howatt realized that the traditional model for understanding organizations was too simple. It obscured key organizational components that are essential for sustainable success (Figure 1).

Through his extensive experience with organizations, Howatt realized that there are five levels at which an organization needs to be functioning effectively if it is to be sustainable. These five levels enable senior leadership to ensure that the talent and operational systems of an organization are truly aligned. The TalOp framework (Figure 2) illustrates these five levels.

While the TalOp methodology is applicable in all forms of organizational analysis, it is particularly helpful in understanding how a CRM plan needs to be adopted across the organization. The TalOp framework serves to remind senior leaders that client satisfaction requires an organization to be fully committed to this in its vision and strategic plan (Level 1), reflected in the systems for managing people and productivity (Level 2), experienced in the organizational culture and climate (Level

# Traditional Metrics

Client Satisfaction

Defined Outputs (Services/Products) Results

Performance Results

Figure 1 — Traditional Metrics

## TalOp's Five Levels

| | | | | | |
|---|---|---|---|---|---|
| **Level 1** Strategic | Organizational Vision & Strategic Plan | + | Defined Employee Expectations & Accountability | = | Defined Performance Expectations & Results |
| **Level 2** People & Process | Required Capabilities for People & Process Outputs | + | Actual Workforce Core Competencies & Defined Processes | = | Workforce's Output Potential Capability |
| **Level 3** Climate & Culture | Desired Culture & Employee Engagement | + | Employee Perception of Culture & Motivation | = | Employee Loyalty, Commitment & Motivation |
| **Level 4** Leadership Effectiveness | Defined Leadership Requirements | + | Actual Skill of Leadership | = | Leadership Capacity to Balance Organizational & Employee Needs |
| **Level 5** Employee Health & Productivity | Employee Perception of Fairness & Control | + | Employee Coping Skills | = | Employee Risk for Counterproduct-ive Behaviours |

Figure 2 — TalOp's Five Levels

3), modeled through its leadership effectiveness (Level 4), and supported through employee health and productivity (Level 5). If an organization is not focused on client service at every level, its ability to sustain excellent client service is at risk.

## All Levels of an Organization Must Adopt CRM Plan

Quality client service requires a motivated team that understands the value of keeping clients satisfied on a daily basis. The goal of the CRM plan is to increase the sense of employee pride and respect for the organization and to define expectations for a quality client experience.

Hearing from organizations that had been disappointed in the long-term impact of CRM efforts, Howatt observed that many organizations look for Band-Aid approaches that do not look to the root cause of their challenges. One organization invested in a pre-packaged customer service program, including fun accessories, posters and video clips, only to find that the up-tick in customer satisfaction didn't last more than a few weeks. Upon closer investigation, it quickly became clear that there was a front-line supervisor who lacked positive communication skills and used sarcasm as the key means of providing feedback. Employees were unable to show much enthusiasm to customers because they weren't enthusiastic about their place of employment.

The impact of CRM is almost entirely dependent upon the engagement of employees. Client service is directly related to staff morale. An engaged staff will be much more open to delivering effective client service than employees who are not content. Therefore, it is advisable to assess the level of employee engagement or commitment and the workplace culture. Figure 3 is a tool you can use as a quick assessment of whether the workplace offers a value proposition to its employees.

## What is Our Employee Value Proposition?
### Product Brand is Only 7%[1] of Why People Come to an Organization

#### 9 Attributes That Influence Employee Value Proposition

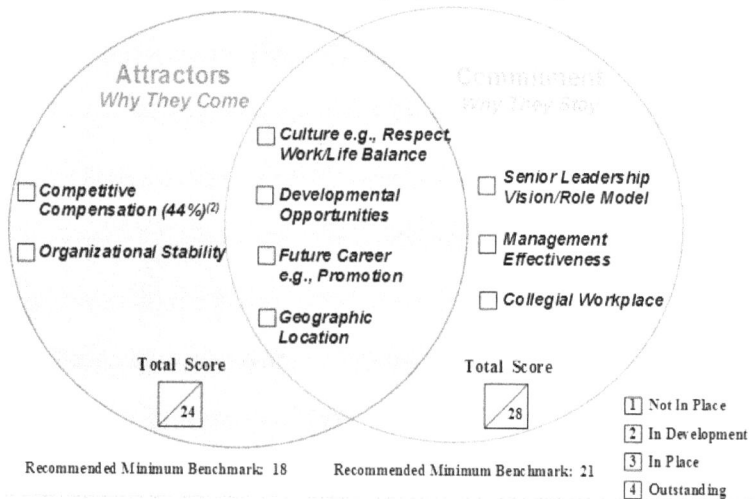

Attractors
Why They Come

Commitment
Why They Stay

☐ Culture e.g., Respect, Work/Life Balance

☐ Competitive Compensation (44%)[2]

☐ Developmental Opportunities

☐ Senior Leadership Vision/Role Model

☐ Organizational Stability

☐ Future Career e.g., Promotion

☐ Management Effectiveness

☐ Collegial Workplace

☐ Geographic Location

Total Score

/24

Total Score

/28

[1] Not In Place
[2] In Development
[3] In Place
[4] Outstanding

Recommended Minimum Benchmark: 18      Recommended Minimum Benchmark: 21

[1] Corporate Leadership Counsel (2007);   [2] Corporate Leadership Counsel (2007)

Figure 3 — Employee Value Proposition

Organizational psychology research suggests that organizations struggling with trust issues between employees and their supervisors are not ripe for a CRM program. When employees trust their employer and believe they are being treated fairly they will be more willing to engage in the types of behaviours required to achieve client service excellence. Employee engagement increases the likelihood that those who serve internal or external clients will buy in to the value and importance of keeping their clients satisfied on a daily basis.

Therefore, before embarking on developing a CRM model, organizations should consider the status of their employee engagement. This often is a weak link in the client relationship supply chain. The success of a CRM program depends on employee motivation and commitment to the organization and its clients. Optimal CRM performance requires employees understanding CRM's importance, and their contribution to client satisfaction. Employees also need to be clear on how a CRM strategy can benefit their day-to-day quality of work life. Employees who embrace the program and show this conviction in the performance of their job responsibilities increase the likelihood of providing both internal and external clients with a high quality experience.

If the assessment tool in Figure 3 suggests that the organization is not quite ready to embark on a CRM exercise, there are several actions the organization can undertake to improve the situation:

- Have a clear, defined vision and plan that tell everyone where the organization is going, and communicate them to all employees.

- Keep communicating the plan and how results are being measured over and over — never worry about too much communication that promotes clarity and direction and shares performance results.

- Eliminate employee role confusion. Ensure employees are clear on their functions and organizational rules. This will promote organizational transparency and set clear expectations and boundaries for all employees.

- Demonstrate a commitment to building trust with the work-force; this will remove unwarranted fears or sense of coercion (particularly important when CRM is being introduced).

- Show employees how their functions are connected and contribute to the organization's overall success.

- Provide employees with an opportunity to receive regular, meaningful feedback on their current status and performance, as well as an opportunity for development and learning.

Paying attention to employee engagement and taking steps to improve relationships within an organization will enable it to have positive relationships with its clients, and to focus on CRM.

## H&H CRM Model

Recognizing that any CRM model needs to be embedded into all five of the TalOp levels of an organization, Howatt worked with Tyler Hayden, an international expert in developing teams and customer service, to create an easy and relevant tool for organizations to do just that. This resulted in the development of the H&H CRM Model. It focuses on developing an organization's internal capacity to engage in quality client relationships. The H&H CRM Model addresses the two pillars of CRM: relationship building and client service. Neither can independently ensure client satisfaction. Together, they offer a practical approach to CRM for any organization:

- *Relationship Building* — Client caretakers (those individuals in the organization who have direct contact with the client) are responsible for creating and maintaining a connection with clients and ensuring that all agreements are kept. Relationships encourage clients to stay, because they have invested in the relationship, and they have confidence in what they can expect from the organization.

- *Client Service* — Effective long-term support of clients, based on ongoing attention and a commitment to service by the entire team. Client service is about keeping the organization's promises (whether tacit or explicit). Client service supports the establishment of new relationships with clients and continuation of the relationship long into the future.

## Relationship Push and Pull

Clients are the raison d'être of most organizations. They not only purchase and consume the products or services, clients also are the best sales force and promoters for recruiting new clients. Therefore, relationship building is vital to the organization. It requires an understanding of the push and pull forces at work in relationships.

A powerful motivator of human behaviour is emotion. Positive experience creates positive emotion that breeds familiarity, confidence, and trust. The *push* refers to actions that push clients and organizations apart. The client or caretaker would prefer not to experience these at all. They are behaviours that are perceived as and come in the form of words, gestures, or actions.

Keep in mind that perception is subjective; different clients and caretakers will have different levels of tolerance for what is and is not acceptable. However, regardless of who perceives the negative, a push moves the interaction away from a positive and can result in an upset client.

The *pull* relationship refers to actions that pull clients and organizations together. Clients and caretakers use these actions to build a trust relationship. Pull elements promote and facilitate the CRM model's success regardless of the service level agreement.

## Case Study

Consider the following example of a pushy client and a supportive caretaker. Whenever the client does not get exactly what they think they should, they become pushy. They demonstrate aggression through their non-verbals, voice volume, and tone. In this push state they challenge the caretaker in a negative manner in the hope of getting what they want. This client keeps getting more and more upset the more they interact and do not hear what they want from the caretaker. This can set the stage for conflict and frustration. The caretaker who tries to be supportive loses their composure and starts to push back. At this point, the client interaction is negative. Regardless of the service level agreement, the relationship between this client and caretaker is strained.

It doesn't matter who started the push. If the tone of the interaction does not become positive, both client and caretaker will walk away with a negative perception. In this case, the obvious risk is that the client will believe they had a poor client service experience; this will affect their future relationship with the caretaker and the organization. The caretaker may also become negative and cold and direct with clients, thinking all clients are going to push them around if they let them. Regardless of who started the push, the client has the final decision to come back or to tell others about their perceptions. The axiom holds true — the client is always right. One negative experience with one caretaker can label an entire group or organization.

A manager's response to an unhappy client can create another push risk for the organization. If a manager hears a client complaint and reacts without getting the facts, the manager may require changes in caretaker response and erode the trust and empowerment of caretakers to deal with clients.

Caretakers will become less willing to try to turn challenging relationships around, and instead pass them along to the manager. This results in inappropriate delegation of their work, and further frustrating the manager as to why staff are not taking ownership of client relations. The caretakers in these situations often become more confused and stressed as to why they have to deal with abusive clients. If, instead, caretakers are coached in a set of skills to manage difficult clients they are not likely to become engaged in a push relationship.

Placing all the blame on caretakers without looking at client interaction can also negatively impact employee loyalty and commitment. Managers need to understand that employees who are not trained to deal with clients will often fall short of expectations, regardless of the service level agreement or CRM model. Training in appropriate skills is key to sustainable client relationship management.

The goal of the H&H CRM Model is to promote positive and proactive *pulling* behaviours. The model can be used to develop a brand new CRM approach or to audit an existing CRM strategy. The key is to have all caretakers able to navigate the push from clients, and use the pull to get clients to a place of acceptance and/or satisfaction.

## Client Service

Good client service starts with employees who feel empowered, energized, and respected. The relationship between front-line management and workers is key to this. Furthermore, managers are the role models for how they want their employees to treat clients. A the boss who is rude to employees is likely to hear complaints about rude customer service. Good managers can promote service excellence in many ways, such as providing:

- clear job description

- employee coaching

- employee personal and professional goals

- employee life planning

- team vision statement

- open communication

- staff training to teach client service

- safe feedback

- role modeling of client service for staff

- staff evolution

Client service is more than being polite and having a good attitude. It also is about being clear on what is being promised to clients and how to fulfill that promise. Effective, long-term support of client service requires commitment to delivering the defined service level agreement (SLA). An SLA can be formal or informal, express or tacit. It spells out exactly what clients can expect, such as response times, service level, consequences for failed service, how success will be defined, and policies and procedures that must be adhered to when providing a service or product.

Client service is supported by information gathered in the relationship building phase. That information should be captured in a client book or database. By setting up databases, keeping track of what a client does, keeping a record of important facts and details, and by constantly asking clients what they want, caretakers can learn more about their clients and treat them differently than others.

Caretakers gain a competitive advantage by making it worth a client's time to teach them about their needs. Once client services have been customized, a competitor cannot offer the same service. If clients are treated well, it's not worth their time to educate alternative suppliers (Capon).

Consistency of service standards also is important. It is part of the brand. It predicts and creates the mindset for expectations, and the attitude of clients: *"I know when I place the order that I won't have to worry;"* or *"I know I'm going to have to fight and argue with them until the project is complete."* When an SLA is not carried out consistently, there is a risk that it will fail to meet clients' needs.Client service research suggests that one upset client can negatively influence up to 12 current or potential clients. This is obviously damaging to an organization's performance results. The goal of a well thought out CRM approach is to mitigate the risk that clients will have a negative experience with caretakers. This also helps prepare caretakers to avoid getting pulled down by negative interaction facilitated by upset clients.

Because of the importance of consistency, CRM should be considered a team effort; all members must have the same level of commitment. Everyone must feel valued and the following factors should be in place or caretakers should have an opportunity to develop them:

- a sense of pride and respect for the organization

- trust and respect for their manager and team leader

- the potential to earn fair compensation

- an affiliation with senior personnel that their work is valued and respected

- an opportunity develop and grow in their present position

CRM takes persistence and commitment by management to implement a plan. Results are spread over a period of time.

# Who Are Clients?

- Clients are the most important people to our business.

- Clients are not dependent upon us; we are interdependent with them.

- Clients are not interruptions to our work; they are the purpose of it.

- Clients are a part of our business; they are not outsiders.

- Clients do us a favour when they call; we are not doing them a favour by serving them.

- Clients are not people to argue or match wits with. No one has ever really won an argument with a client.

- Clients bring us their problems, needs, and dreams. We want to help them solve their problems, meet their needs, and realize their dreams.

- Clients are deserving of the most courteous, attentive, and professional service we can give them at all times.

- Clients are the lifeblood of this and every other business.

- Clients are our past, our present, and our future.

- Clients can be both internal and external; it is important for caretakers to know who their clients are and what they expect.

# CHAPTER 2

# The ABCs of CRM

Applying the relationship building and client service pillars to the organization, Howatt and Hayden developed the H&H CRM framework (Figure 4). It is intended to assist managers to design, develop, and implement their own CRM plan.

When framing a CRM approach, it is vital to ensure that it is consistent with an organization's values and culture. The three columns represent the three Cs: *Client, Company, and Caretaker*, with the CRM addressing the three aspects of their contributions to the client relationship management plan. These roles form the hierarchy of ABCs:

**A** elements refer to the heart (impact of emotions).

**B** elements refer to the head (impact of thinking out the details to achieve success).

**C** elements refer to the hands (impact of behavioural actions).

Each of these columns will be considered in turn.

## Client ABCs

**Attitude** — Not all clients are the same. It can be challenging for a caretaker to do a formal assessment as to what a client's communication preference is or to fully understand their personality. Caretakers need to

| Client | Company | Caretaker |
|---|---|---|
| **Attitude**<br><br>% ideal<br><br>% passive<br><br>% aggressive | **Attitude**<br><br>$ invested in CRM training<br><br>Time invested in CRM | **Assessment**<br><br>Strengths<br><br>Emotional triggers<br><br>Communication preferences |
| **Benchmark Expectations**<br><br>Same-day delivery<br><br>Free delivery<br><br>Plug n Play | **Boundaries**<br><br>What is beyond what can be delivered/promised?<br><br>CRM Roles | **'Bilities**<br><br>Self-management<br><br>Communication<br><br>Product knowledge<br><br>Initiative |
| **Consequence**<br><br>% highly satisfied<br><br>% new business through referrals | **Capacity**<br><br>What measures<br><br>What benchmarks | **Choice Facilitator**<br><br>Scope of recommendations |

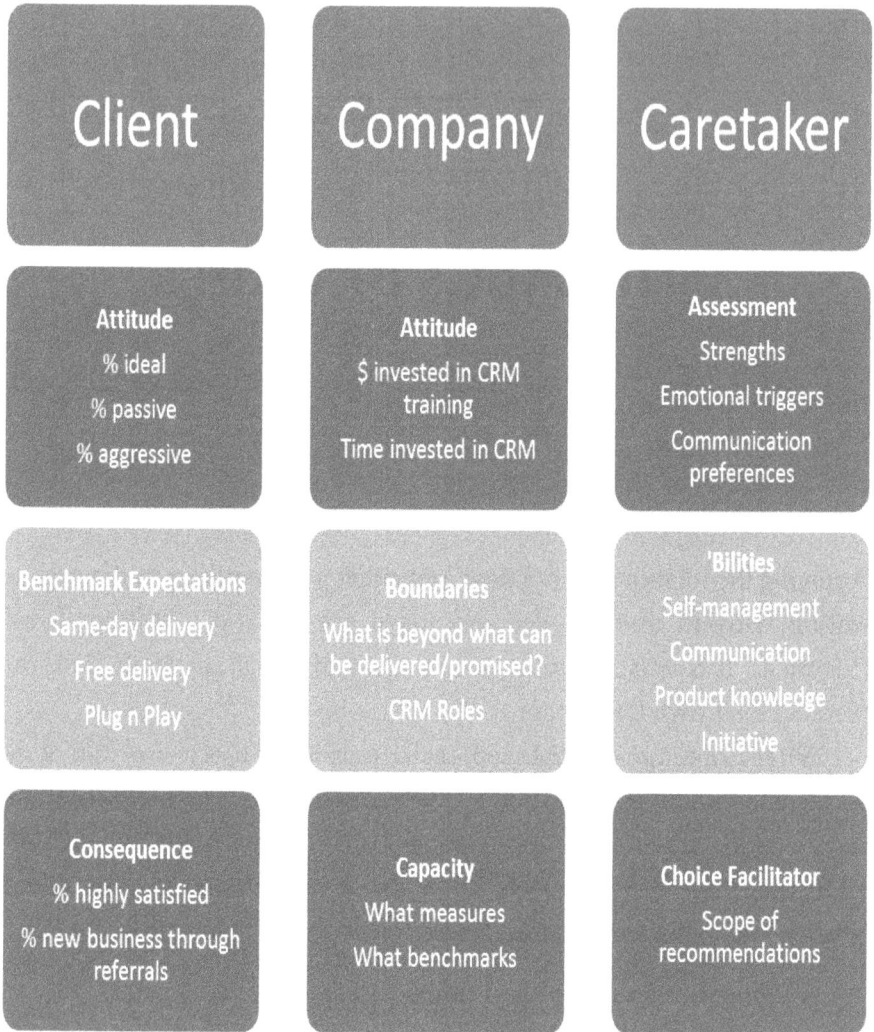

Figure 4 — H&H CRM Framework

be aware of behavioural forces that pull relationships together and push them apart.

One strategy for understanding the different types of clients is to consider how most clients can fit into one of three categories, and in each category a client can fall on a continuum from low to high tendencies:

- The first type — the ideal clients — exhibit natural pull characteristics, being good spirited people who are kind, patient, and grateful. They know what they need and can clearly articulate it. This is the vast majority of clients. Most people want to get along and be respectful. If the caretaker avoids push behaviour, there is a high likelihood of positive interaction.

- The second type of client is passive. The challenge with a passive client is that they may not ask for what they really want and may become frustrated (they may not be sure about what they want themselves). Extremely passive clients may assume that caretakers are too busy or have more important things to do than to provide them with service or support. As a result, these clients never actually ask for help. This may be the result of having a negative experience with a caretaker who was aggressive (pusher) and, wanting to avoid direct conflict, the client doesn't ask for assistance. Sometimes these clients have internal expectations, such as getting help within three minutes and if no one comes to their aid then they decide that there is a lack of service. In these situations, the client perceives something is not right for them, and there is a good chance the caretaker may never know that the client is upset. As a result, this type of client may never complain to the caretaker directly; they may only complain to others that the service was poor. This can be the most challenging type of client, because the caretaker does not know that they need to make something right. However, the caretaker can improve the likelihood of a positive outcome by avoiding making assumptions, and asking the client to validate the caretaker's understanding of their needs. Being patient and warm with these clients may help overcome their reticence to voice their concerns so that the caretaker can determine if and how they can help. Furthermore, outlining service options and regularly checking with the client to see if they have questions will improve the likelihood of more informative communications.

- The third type of client is the abusive client who believes that by taking an extremely aggressive style they will receive a better deal, and get more attention. The caretaker needs to quickly assess whether the aggressive client is intentionally trying to manipulate the relationship, or whether they are outraged because of a poor experience and can be turned into an ideal client. Should the interaction not get turned around, it is important that the caretaker always maintain a professional demeanor and comply with the service standards set by the organization (which should include how to close off a conversation with an irate/abusive client).

**Benchmark Clients' Expectations** — *Preferences.* Much like personality type, every client has their own set of expectations as to what they think they need with respect to service level. How well an organization has defined and educated both its clients and caretakers on its service level agreements will influence clients' expectations. Not every client will have a clear picture of what they want as a deliverable, but most will have a clear expectation as to how they want to be treated. Client expectations are influenced by individual preferences that are learned from previous experiences, or come from interpretations of some policy, or even the law (e.g., government safety standard). Most clients will expect a positive experience with a helpful and caring caretaker.

*Assumptions:* An important step when developing any CRM model is to make a commitment to remove assumptions. Never assume what a client wants; be committed to understanding what they expect and the facts as they see them. The caretaker needs to be skilled at asking open-ended questions, and to being patient in engaging the client in a conversation to get their facts. A best practice is to understand the client's point of view and rationale before ever saying no.

*Interest:* More than anything, most clients want to know that the caretaker is interested in learning what they want and why. A caretaker may not be able to give a client exactly what they want. However, through a positive interaction where the client believes they are being listened to, whatever alternative outcome that the caretaker can offer often will be enough.

**Consequence** — Whether they realize it or not, clients keep an internal scorecard of what they perceive as being positive or negative interactions with caretakers. Caretakers will have greater success when they understand that a client has two measures: 1) how they believe they were treated, and 2) how the caretaker assisted them to get what they wanted. This defines how they believe the caretaker's service level has assisted them, and will ultimately define the CRM model's success.

Clients vote with their feet; unhappy clients often say nothing and stop using a service, or use it only as a last alternative. Clients who believe a caretaker is committed to providing quality service will be more tolerant of not getting what they want, and more empathetic of a caretaker's position, as they are often just the messenger. When a client develops this sense of loyalty to a caretaker they will return and become one of the caretaker's biggest fans and referral sources.

To achieve a high level of client satisfaction, caretakers do not need to give clients what they want regardless of the ask, but they always need the client to perceive that they have been treated as a person. Knowing that a client's measure of service can be either positive or negative is important in facilitating long-term relationships with them. Each organization when developing a CRM program will need to determine how it is going to get feedback from clients with respect to how they perceive and evaluate the quality of service they are receiving.

## Company ABCs

**Attitude Alignment** — A well thought out CRM approach is based on a client service vision of excellence that is directly linked to an organization's value statement. However, as the old saying goes, talk is cheap. A CRM approach to work requires more than talk; it requires action and follow-through. Attitude is illustrated by actions. Investing in a CRM model requires resources and time to implement. Management needs to define the size of budget, time, and resources that will be put towards the model. A thoughtful CRM model empowers caretakers to make decisions and take necessary action to help clients get their needs met.

If senior leadership adheres to a command and control approach that does not trust or allow caretakers to use their creativity and problem solving skills, the CRM approach will not achieve its full potential. Both clients and caretakers will get frustrated if the common response to a reasonable request is, *"I'm sorry, this is a policy; there's nothing I can do to help."* What clients want to see is a caretaker who is able to explore with them what may be possible and to take action.

Even if a client ultimately ends up with a no, if they believe their request was put through a decision making process this often will promote goodwill and acceptance. Obviously, outrageous requests from angry clients would not warrant the same level of diligence. However, many times an over-the-top request can be broken down into component parts, some of which may be possible to address.

The key to a successful CRM approach is senior management support. Senior management must not just delegate CRM; they need to be engaged and involved so caretakers see the importance of their work, that there are resources to make it happen, and to follow up on CRM results.

**Boundaries and Service Level Agreements** — When developing an organization's CRM approach, an important step is establishing the details with respect to who will do what, when, and how. Before a service level agreement can be developed, management must make it clear what functions caretakers are providing that will be part of it, as well as what knowledge and skills are required to support its implementation.

To clearly understand the specifics behind the knowledge and skills required to perform a CRM strategy, a best practice will include developing core competencies that support it. The CRM core competency will define the type of training and development needed to ensure caretakers have the knowledge and skills to deal with clients.

It is recommended that management include key stakeholders within an organization when developing service level agreements and CRM core competencies. A core competency profile can be used to recruit and select new hires. On-boarding programs can be helpful in ensuring all new hires have insight on policies and procedures required to perform caretakers' defined functions.

**Capacity** — Once a CRM approach has been implemented and is operational, organizations need to be clear on what metrics and monitors will be used to track CRM results internally. This step promotes caretaker accountability and enables an organization to predict whether the service level will meet client expectations. These kinds of measures help management evaluate current capacity in CRM and can be benchmarked against client feedback to evaluate how well internal metrics are working.

# Caretaker ABCs

**Assessment**— Caretakers need to be aware of their own communication preferences. Like clients, caretakers have their own personality types, so it's helpful for them to be aware of their personality and communication styles and to develop insight into their communication and personality preferences with respect to how they carry on conversations. This insight can help them better match a client's communication style. It will also strengthen relationships with their team and align their actions to the organization's commitment to its service level of excellence.

Caretakers should be given an opportunity to explore how these preferences can positively facilitate push or pull behaviours within the team or with their clients. There is no right or wrong; this is about empowerment. It is important for caretakers to discover that people can think and communicate differently and at the same time achieve the same goal.

How effectively each caretaker is able to manage their own personality and follow a defined service level agreement will define an organization's capacity to deliver its CRM approach. And the proficiency of caretakers' CRM core competencies will impact how effectively they can gain a sense of trust from clients — the foundation for long-term client satisfaction.

**'Bilities** — A CRM strategy is more effective when it does not assume that all caretakers have the skills needed to perform at the standard set by management. The CRM plan should include a means for developing or improving these competencies.

To develop CRM core competencies, managers can give caretakers a detailed job handoff document that outlines the knowledge and skills needed to perform their functions and service level agreements. Some of the not-so-obvious benefits of assisting caretakers to acquire these skills are their well-being, happiness, and retention in their roles. Not having the right skills can be stressful, especially when dealing with an upset client. It can lead to conflict and self-doubt, which can negatively impact self-esteem and job satisfaction. This, in turn, affects caretakers' ability to deal positively with clients. Teaching caretakers core competencies not only benefits clients, but also caretakers.

**Choice Facilitator** — Meeting clients' needs often requires a calm and focused approach, such as:

1.  listening

2.  exploring options

3.  assisting clients to understand the obvious and not-so-obvious pros and cons of each option

4.  supporting clients to make decisions

5.  agreeing on decisions

6.  creating an action plan

7.  taking action

This seven-step process clearly does not need to be used in all client interactions, but it provides a process for facilitating pull and helps caretakers know where they are in the process. This keeps them on course and helps them stay focused on pull strategies.

The goal of this process is for caretakers to take clear and concise steps with clients to plot what can be done to meet a client's needs. The client will ultimately determine if they are satisfied with the solution and level of service. While they may not be happy with the solution, they may be happy with the level and care of service that may help them resolve their differences and bring them back. In some cases, though, regardless of what a caretaker does, a client may not be satisfied, to the point where it is clear that they are being unreasonable.

Caretakers require a framework that explains the expectations as to how the CRM approach will be monitored and measured. The caretakers' performance management model will provide the formal feedback indicating whether they performed to required standards and are able to stay on track with clients. The review process provides a framework to evaluate how caretakers are able to apply their CRM core competencies and stay focused on pull strategies.

By addressing its expectations in each of the nine squares in the H&H framework, the organization will have developed its CRM strategy. This should be done initially at the senior level and then workshopped with key client caretakers and culture influencers within the organization, identifying milestones and benchmarking performance to track the progress of the organization on its path to CRM excellence.

# 12 Things Every Client Wants

- Clients want your product and/or service to work for them.

- Clients want to feel good that your solution is the best for their present needs.

- Clients want you to follow up and do what you say you will.

- Clients want you to honour all agreements, big and little.

- Clients want you to be honest and ethical.

- Clients want you to be patient and educate them.

- Clients want you to tell them how you came up with your solutions.

- Clients want to know all the facts.

- Clients want you to be clear about time and cost.

- Clients want you to be responsive to their changes.

- Clients want to be a priority and get special treatment.

- Clients want to know you are an expert.

# CHAPTER 3

# CRM and Caretakers

While CRM involves everyone in the organization, typically there are specific individuals or roles that have direct contact with clients. These are the client caretakers. Caretakers usually consist of sales and marketing staff, customer service agents, and those involved in after-care, such as the contact person in the maintenance or warranty office. Those who provide internal services to other employees also are caretakers. The end goal of any CRM plan is to influence caretakers to build and maintain long and healthy relationships with clients.

Client service is based on a simple premise: Clients want a caretaker to be respectful, interested in them, and clear as to what the caretaker can and cannot do. Caretakers should be prepared to listen, answer questions, and know their product. When the client believes that the caretaker has the necessary expertise to do what they say they can, the caretaker has trust competence. Caretaker trust competence is achieved through knowing the features of the product: superior service, product quality, uniquely tailored products or services, innovative features, strong brand names, or the strength of the distributor network. This trust competence is a key success driver for any caretaker.

Another key success driver for caretakers is the ability to build and maintain relationships. As indicated by the H&H CRM Model (Figure 4), dealing with client emotions is a key skill of caretakers. The irony is that in order to deal effectively with client emotions, the caretaker must learn to not become emotional themselves, and yet to be able to empathize with the needs of the client. The best CRM caretakers achieve this by being great listeners. By hearing out a client's story, the caretaker has an opportunity to discover what lies beneath the emotion, to hear out the facts and concerns, and to recognize that most negative reactions arise from fear: fear of not being taken seriously, fear of being cheated, fear of not being respected or valued.

The very act of hearing out a client is, in itself, an act of respect. For the ideal client and the passive client, it is a pleasant gift. For the upset client, it may be a welcome surprise that someone will actually hear them out.

Two types of client relationships influence the CRM design:

- *Transactional Relationships:* A client pays for a service that can be a one-time interaction, or intermittent interaction that occurs whenever a client requires the service or product being provided.

- *Strategic Partner Relationships:* An example is a vendor agreement where an external client is working with a part of an organization providing a service for a specific period of time. These relationships can also be developed within an organization when one part provides an ongoing service to another, such as IT support security.

While client relationship building is important in any context, where there is potential for repeat business, or extended contact in completing the transaction, the caretaker's relationship building skills become even more important.

In either case, the issue is not about trying to get a client to want what the seller has, but rather first understanding what the client wants and needs, and then showing how the seller's offering satisfies those needs. The "product" is best presented as a solution that will satisfy the client's needs. The key is to ensure that the buyer is being offered what they want. Once the client is convinced that they can get what they want, the next important issue is to ensure that all client service agreements are kept.

By focusing on the relationship rather than the sale, the caretaker is in a better position to deepen the connection with the client and establish rapport that will have the effect of strengthening the likelihood of the sale, the recommendation, or return customer. A useful exercise for establishing that rapport is "Steps To Yes."

## Steps to Yes

1.  After listening to the client's needs, the caretaker reframes what was shared and asks if the client agrees with that summation of the issue (the first yes).

2.  The caretaker discusses the options for what is needed to address the issue, and again closes that portion of the conversation with agreement (the second yes).

3.  The caretaker engages in a discussion about what the organization can offer that will solve all or part of the problem and obtain subsequent agreements about what will help (more yeses).

This model of the conversation builds momentum. If at any point the client raises a roadblock or an uncertainty, the caretaker has an opportunity to understand what the client needs in order to make a decision, and whether the caretaker can help the client get the information needed. Building the relationship is a valuable investment. It not only supports the sales effort, it also gathers lots of useful information about the client's needs, and shows the client that the caretaker truly cares about their needs. This transforms a sales effort into a client care effort.

The information gathered in the relationship building phase also enables the organization to better understand the context of the client's needs and how much to invest in serving different segments of the potential client pool. Christensen and Raynor suggest that organizations need to think differently about their clients and CRM by identifying clients who are high maintenance (those who drain the profit margin because their expectations do not align with the organization's promises) and those whose expectations are aligned with the organization's brand. Consider a client who wants a high performance vehicle but who wants to use it in off-road competitions and complains of the maintenance costs, versus the client who understands the market, the product, and their needs. Successful organizations educate clients in the products and services available, and enable them to determine whether they are the right fit.

It is important to consider clients' buying decision processes. A CRM strategy may be focused on providing high client experience, strong product commitment policies that back the product, and outstanding service and follow-up, but some clients make their buying decisions solely on price. Those clients may not be easy to retain. The conversation needs to move from price to value.

Christensen and Raynor found that a current client is a valuable client because they have invested in the relationship. They do not need reasons to stay, and are likely to stay unless an experience creates a push for them to leave. They are more likely to stick with a provider of quality service than risk being exposed to a new service provider that is not yet proven or does not have a clear understanding of their needs and situation. This type of client has come to believe and trust in the product or service that often can lead to a long-term, loyal relationship.

### Dealing With An Outraged Client

The first role of a caretaker is to try to put themselves in the role of the client and have some empathy. The caretaker should pause and listen to the client's story. Sometimes a quiet ear to an upset client will lower their anxiety, especially if they believe that the caretaker really cares and is trying to be helpful. If the person is rude or disrespectful, the caretaker can simply say something like, "I'm here to help. It's clear that you are upset. What will help both of us is for me to listen to your story so that I can understand the issue and what you want. Does this make sense?"

Many times a frustrated person may project their frustrations onto the caretaker, when in fact they are not frustrated with the person but with the situation. By listening and reframing what the client is saying to ensure understanding of the issue, the caretaker will quickly be able to discern if there is an opportunity to shift the tone of the conversation to a problem-solving level, or whether this is a situation where the client is intentionally using aggression. These are rare instances, as most clients do want to have a positive relationship. Most clients will be able to dial-back their emotional levels when they realize that the caretaker wants to understand their concern.

## Dealing With An Abusive Client

No caretaker should be expected to take verbal abuse of any kind or deal with an irresponsible and angry person, as there is no reasoning in this context, and it is only an opportunity for escalation.

Regardless of how much a caretaker may attempt to meet an abusive client's needs, some are clear pushers on a mission. Unfortunately, abusive clients may have learned to get what they want through losing their cool. In every client interaction, caretakers need only focus on being responsible and committed to providing fair and consistent client service with a focus on pulling behaviours (e.g., being friendly, non-aggressive, and listening), and never need to take abuse.

Senior leaders need to be clear that they have a no-tolerance policy for abuse by clients or caretakers. There is never an excuse for disrespect and showing anger to a client. When a client is being abusive, the caretaker should politely disengage from the conversation. Caretakers are not helping when they participate in unacceptable behaviour such as telling off a client. Managers should enforce this expectation consistently. Employees who are not committed to good client service may require some coaching or even discipline if they do not accept responsibility for poor behaviour and continue to act in a manner that could be harmful to their organization or a client.

Simply having a no-tolerance policy will not help caretakers develop the skills for dealing with challenging clients. When designing a CRM model, management cannot assume that all caretakers have the skills, when hired, to manage difficult clients. Caretakers can be more effective if they are oriented to and become aware of the different types of clients, as well as different approaches they can use to facilitate a positive and safe interaction with clients.

## In Closing

Caretakers are the face of the organization. Their behaviour and skills in client relationship management create the brand. Therefore, it is imperative that caretakers be given clear direction on the organization's expectations with respect to their mandate for dealing with clients, how far they can go in problem solving, and how they can respectfully disengage in the rare circumstance of an abusive client.

# Tips for Caretakers

- Be attentive to your client's needs. The key for good client service is to LISTEN, LISTEN, LISTEN, LISTEN to what your client NEEDS.

- The basis for client relationship management is charisma, because it is charisma rather than a product's qualities that makes the sale with high-end services or products.

- Be patient, kind, and polite.

- The motto, "The client is always right in knowing what they want" may not always be true, but it is a good place to start.

- When working with people, look at them as individuals who want nothing more than the chance to make a decision to buy your product or service.

- Value is what converts a sale, not price. The cost of your product or service will not usually be the final determinant if the client buys once or many times.

- Create a positive emotional response. The ability to create experiences that are positive for your clients will be the key to CRM, selling products and increasing your market share.

- Set the atmosphere. Clients like it when you create an ambiance that is appealing and inviting, such as background music, fish tanks, nice smells, pictures, video, etc. Create an environment so the client feels they are getting value from just coming into your space.

- The extra mile: Clients like to be treated like royalty — we all do. When we work to serve the client's needs, and give them a good experience, they will be back to visit — and to buy.

- The key to quality client service is the environment, so be aware of it, and focus on providing an environment that reflects quality.

# Tips for Keeping Clients

- Meet your client with a smile, and acknowledge them within 15 seconds. Clients appreciate a warm welcome and the acknowledgment that they matter. The faster this is done, the quicker the rapport is set up. If you can't see them now, tell them how long you will be, and stick to that time. Don't be pushy; be genuine and real.

- Keep a smile on your face at all times when meeting your clients. (Even if you are speaking by phone or e-chatting, the smile on your face influences your tone, voice, and thinking pattern.) Also, be mindful of your eyes. Look your client in the eyes if they are looking at you. If they seem uncomfortable, look away and break the perceived tension by making a simple statement such as, *"Welcome. If you need anything, just ask. I will be over there."* It is important that the client feels welcomed and engaged on their terms. However, some may be a bit introverted and may want to be left alone to determine what they may want to ask about or buy.

- Always make first contact in a non-threatening manner. Your first words should be to help them relax, like an icebreaker. Avoid pressure questions or quick sales talk. Use a simple phrase like, *"Hello (smiling), how can I help you, sir/miss?"* or *"Hello (smiling) my name is John, can I be of service to you today?"*

- Be attentive, and listen for what the client needs — and help them obtain it. Set the stage for safe communication.

- Be well prepared in regard to how you look, and to how your area of work is set up. It is important to look professional at all times — your appearance really does matter. Your clients will evaluate your appearance; some will be more judgmental than others. If you look sharp, people will treat you the way you look. So always be ready. Your work area also needs to be well maintained. Ask yourself, *"Would I want to be a client in this space?"*

# Tips for Keeping Clients (cont'd)

- When you talk to a client on the phone, ensure you are clear and concise. Because your client cannot see you, the only thing you have to make an impression is your voice tone, speed, and volume. The keys to be successful on the phone are as follows:

  ◊ Provide your client with a greeting.

  ◊ Identify yourself by name.

  ◊ If you need to put a client on hold, ask for permission, and wait to receive it. Make sure you tell them how long you will be, and get back to them in that time — people hate being on hold.

  ◊ Match your client's speed, tone, volume, and pitch (provided they are not upset and yelling).

  ◊ Use your client's language and key words in your replies.

  ◊ Ask the client an action question, such as, *"How can I help you today?"* to get to the point.

  ◊ If you need to call back to meet the client's needs, be specific as to when, and how long you'll be — and ensure you call back.

  ◊ Always thank your client for calling.

## Fast Focus Measure — Client Service

Below is a quick self-assessment tool for caretakers that can benchmark client service behaviours and monitor trends. The tool also serves a second purpose by educating/reminding the caretaker of the organization's client service expectations.

Circle NT if not true; T if sometimes true; VT if very true.
Total your score.

| NT T VT | Statements |
|---|---|
| 1  2  3 | 1. I promote meeting clients with a smile and model this. |
| 1  2  3 | 2. I promote the importance of good phone skills. |
| 1  2  3 | 3. I ensure client service is a major part of staff training. |
| 1  2  3 | 4. I do not expect staff to have all the skills, so we train them. |
| 1  2  3 | 5. We model exactly what we want for client service. |
| 1  2  3 | 6. I ensure the environment is appealing to the client. |
| 1  2  3 | 7. I promote staff wellness so they feel good about themselves so they can better interact with the client. |
| 1  2  3 | 8. I have clear boundaries of no tolerance for unethical behaviour with clients. |
| 1  2  3 | 9. I monitor client service by getting feedback with client surveys. |
| 1  2  3 | 10. I want our staff to be the best in this area, and will accept nothing less. |
|  | The higher your score, the greater your competency in this area. This is an awareness activity to help identify some areas of need. |
| **TOTALS** | Howatt HR Consulting Inc. © 2004 | licensed use only |

## Universal Client Feedback Processor

*It is important to discuss potential client issues and to develop a glossary of positive responses. Below are some positive alternatives for handling difficult client situations.*

| Client Statement<br>Avoid Negative Words/Phrases | Suggested Responses<br>Use Positive Language |
|---|---|
| X **Double negatives:** No trouble, I don't disagree, not bad, certainly not, no problem, do not hesitate to, etc.<br><br>X **Defensive words:** It's not my responsibility, that's not the way we do it, that won't work, we're pleased to, we regret that . . ., we hope this answers your questions, etc.<br><br>X **Challenging language:** If what you say is true, we must have your answer by ..., we are doing this with the understanding that . . ., we can't do that, etc.<br><br>X **Patronizing language:** Because you are an important client, since you neglected to . . ., we can't understand how you came to that conclusion, we fail to see the importance, etc. | • Our information suggests a different viewpoint<br><br>• We can help you _____, if you provide us with _____<br><br>• We can provide you with _____ within [hours/days] after we receive _____ from you.<br><br>• Here are some suggestions to make that work<br><br>• Specifically, we offer [list services/products]<br><br>• This matter is important. We'll do our best to deal with it appropriately.<br><br>• In that situation, we might have come up with a different solution.<br><br>• We intend to respond aggressively to your concerns. |
| X We need _____ now! | • That certainly is urgent. We can put it ahead of _____ and have it done by _____. |
| X The research you sent me is old. I want the current facts. | • The report we sent was the best available information. I will check for further updates and get back to you by [specific time/day]. |

## Universal Client Feedback Processor (cont'd)

*It is important to discuss potential client issues and to develop a glossary of positive responses. Below are some positive alternatives for handling difficult client situations.*

| Client Statement<br>Avoid Negative Words/Phrases | Suggested Responses<br>Use Positive Language |
| --- | --- |
| X  You promised me new data by noon. It's already 2 o'clock. | • You're right, [use name].<br><br>• My records show that we are experiencing a [specific time frame] delay because of _____; OR<br><br>• I will check the status now and get back to you by [specific time]. |
| X  Your competitor is giving our competitor _____.<br><br>X  I'm not so sure that the strategy we discussed is working well. Maybe we should try something else. | • Our emphasis is on _____ and we think that is a unique value-add in your specific situation.<br><br>• That's one option. We're known for our expertise in _____ and we believe that this solution is a great one.<br><br>  ◊  Let's look at the facts more carefully . . .; OR<br><br>  ◊  What would be a good time for [senior person's name] to get back to you to discuss your idea? |

# CHAPTER 4

# Establishing Client Confidence

Client relationship management is about instilling confidence in your client that your organization will deliver on its promises. Credibility is the key to the whole market-positioning process (Gitomer). It instills confidence that your organization is the right partner for serving a need. McKenna identified three stages to building credibility:

- *Inference.* When a client orders from a pizza place that has a reputation for making outstanding pizza they believe they will be getting an outstanding pizza, based on past experience.

- *Reference.* Analysts, retailers, journalists, and clients all talk to one another and spread word about a product or service provided by a company or individual that displays competence in their field. Be active in managing the message being sent out to the public.

- *Evidence.* No matter how great your credentials or how much experience you've had, people pay more attention to what others have to say about you. Use case studies to tell what you did for whom and the difference it made in their business.

## What is Trust Competence?

Trust competence can be defined as the client's belief that you have the necessary expertise to do what you say you can. To get this you must have a relationship that is built on respect and trust. Superior service, better product quality, uniquely tailored products or services, innovative features, strong brand names, or the strength of your distributor network may achieve a differentiated position on competence. Capitalizing on your core competencies or correcting your areas of weakness may internally drive it, or it may be externally driven by quick responses to client needs or competitor developments.

Mutual trust is a shared belief that a caretaker and client can depend on each other to achieve a common purpose. This is the goal of client relationship management. Trust is a primary focus and is managed closely. To have this, both parties must have a sense of:

- *Benevolence:* A belief that one party will act in the interests of the other

- *Honesty:* A belief that the other party will be credible

- *Competence:* A belief that the other party has the necessary expertise

The development of trust is an investment in relationship building that has a long-term payoff. It may take years to build the kind of trust a corporation needs to become a client. Knowing and trusting are two different accomplishments.

Trust emerges as parties share experiences and interpret and assess each other's motives. As they learn more about each other, risk and doubt are reduced. When trust exists between partners, both are motivated to invest in the relationship.

- Calculus-based trust is present in early stages of a relationship and related to economic value. The outcomes of creating and sustaining a new relationship are weighted against those of dissolving it.

- Knowledge-based trust relies on parties' interactive history and knowledge of each other, allowing each to make predictions about the other.

- Identification-based trust happens when mutual understanding is such that each party can act as a substitute for the other in interpersonal interaction. This is found in the latter stages of relationship development.

The goal of client relationship management is to manage trust. It requires the building of trust, which embodies competence that is a component of credibility. Trust is the expectancy that people can rely on another's word. It is built through integrity and consistency in relationships.

Use the simple tool below to assess the trust level you have with someone. Look at a relationship in terms of an emotional bank account, or how much credit (or debit) of goodwill exists between you and your client.

## Client Relationship Dos and Don'ts

*Every relationship has an "emotional bank account." To evaluate the level of trust in a current client relationship, add the number of positive actions currently being practiced. Then subtract the number of negatives currently being practiced. Use the final total to assess how much credit (or debit) of goodwill exists between you and your client.*

| Positive Actions | Negative Actions |
|---|---|
| Initiate positive phone calls | Make only callbacks |
| Make recommendations | Make justifications |
| Use candid language | Use accommodative language |
| Use phone | Use correspondence |
| Show appreciation | Wait for misunderstandings |
| Make service suggestions | Wait for service requests |
| Use "we" problem-solving language | Use "owe us" legal language |
| Get to problems | Respond only to problems |
| Use jargon or shorthand | Use long-winded communications |
| Air personality problems | Hide personality problems |
| Talk of "our future together" | Talk about making good on the past |
| Accept responsibility | Shift blame |
| Plan the future | Rehash the past |

## The Language of Trust

*Consistent references to the strengths you have already identified convey confidence and build client trust. In addition to eliminating weak language when preparing a pitch, take the time to consider what negative questions may be asked and the confident responses you can give.*

- Avoid negative words (e.g., not, can't, but):

  ◊ *Defensive Response:* We may not be the biggest computer store in town, but we can offer you better personal attention than others.

  ◊ *Trust-Building Statement:* Our size enables us to provide clients with a high personal touch experience.

- Avoid bringing up a competitor's name.

  ◊ *Defensive Response:* We do not have as large a selection of computer equipment as some of our competitors, but we specialize in a few brands.

  ◊ *Trust-Building Statement:* We have deep expertise in the computer products we offer. I have been a sales professional with this firm for 10 years and our team has over 100 years of experience.

- Try to answer all questions with an affirming word or phrase (e.g., yes, you are right, that's an interesting point).

  ◊ *Defensive Response:* No, this product was not in the last recall; it has no impact on us, but we have had problems with this manufacturer before.

  ◊ *Trust-Building Statement:* Yes, your facts are correct. We are aware of the issue and are confident that the products we have are reliable.

- Use silence as a sign of confidence. Asking for a moment to consider a question is better than rushing to respond and giving a less than thoughtful response.

- If you don't know the answer to a question, offer to get back to the client rather than giving incorrect information that can destroy your credibility. Never guess.

## Strategies for Building Client Trust

- Know your business, the products, and the competition. Be the best source of information your client can find.

- Ensure your body language is open, positive, and engaging. 90% of what you say will be interpreted through non-verbal communication and you have on average 60 seconds to make an impression.

- Assess your strengths and weaknesses and make a commitment to fill gaps. Identify what additional information and experience you need in core skills. Then make a detailed plan to take the courses, obtain missing credentials, or look for a mentor to get practical experience.

- Develop a clear and credible verbal resume. Be prepared to tell people who you are and what you can do well. Have your evidence ready to support all statements.

- Collect evidence and research that supports your position. Use hypothetical cases, visual aids, real personal experiences and anecdotes, demonstrations, expert and client testimony, statistics, comparisons, and facts and figures that strengthen your image as an industry or product expert.

- Build a living portfolio that supports your expertise. Continually update your record of experience. Your portfolio should be a living document that represents all of your accomplishments to date.

- Continue to self-evaluate your development and expertise. What are the most common problems you face? What mistakes do people make over and over again? What do people perceive themselves as needing? What works? What doesn't? Why?

- Stay current with new terminology. Look for useful and meaningful metaphors, stories, and examples that produce results. This shows your understanding and synthesis of the topic area.

- Make it worth the client's time to teach you about their needs. Once you've customized your services, a competitor cannot offer the same service and, if you treat clients well, it is not worth their time to educate competitors to compete with you. To stay ahead of the competition:
  - ◊ Set up databases.
  - ◊ Keep track of what a client does.
  - ◊ Keep a record of important facts and details.
  - ◊ Constantly ask them what they want by asking them if anything has changed — new lines, new size, new technology. People love to talk about themselves.

## Client Service Model

### Set Service Standards

| Action Steps | Questions |
|---|---|
| 1. Determine the values that are most important to the organization and set service goals.<br>2. Agree on a common language of terms and phrases.<br>3. Define common client issues.<br>4. Delineate the actions to be taken by various team members when issues arise.<br>5. Assess the caretaker's hard and soft skills and decide what training is needed. | • What is a client?<br>• How can we improve our service?<br>• Which issues come up frequently?<br>• What is our escalation policy?<br>• What skills should we develop to meet our goals? |

### Develop Communication Protocols

| Action Steps | Questions |
|---|---|
| 1. Assess current horizontal and vertical communication.<br>2. Determine best methods and frequency for internal communication (e.g., e-mail, meetings, phone, newsletter; daily, weekly, monthly).<br>3. Define procedures and response time for client communication (e.g., scripts, on-line logs; 15 min., 30 min., 24 hrs.).<br>4. Develop a procedure for conducting meetings and agree on frequency. | • Where can we improve our horizontal and vertical communication?<br>• How can we ensure that our responses to clients are consistent?<br>• How often do we need team meetings?<br>• Are we accessible enough to our clients?<br>• How quickly can we reasonably get follow-up answers to our clients in common situations (e.g., simple updates, procedural questions, strategy questions, reports)?<br>• What are the best ways for us to assure that our responses are clear, accurate, and current? |

## Client Service Model (cont'd)

### □Maintain the Information Flow

| Action Steps | Questions |
|---|---|
| 1. Decide on tracking methods (e.g., on-line logs, e-mails, meeting notes).<br>2. Develop necessary forms, scripts, programs, etc.<br>3. Determine who is responsible for updating the various sources of information.<br>4. Assess which caretakers should initiate contact with clients and how frequently. | • What are the best ways for us to access current data immediately?<br>• How can we capture anecdotal information about our clients?<br>• Who should maintain our data?<br>• Which team members should reach out to our clients, how should they contact them, and how frequently should they contact them? |

### Monitor and Evaluate Service

| Action Steps | Questions |
|---|---|
| 1. Develop a procedure for evaluating the administrative process.<br>2. Determine methods for getting client feedback on products, services, and responsiveness.<br>3. Develop a procedure for evaluating and updating protocols and procedures.<br>4. Assess caretakers' skills on a regular basis and explore ways to improve skills/offer additional training. | • How often should we ask for client feedback?<br>• Is our team evaluation effective and a 360 review?<br>• What services can we add?<br>• What training would be a value-add for our clients?<br>• What protocols and procedures work best?<br>• What protocols and procedures should be improved? |

# REFERENCES

Buttle, F. (2004). *Client relationship management*. Oxford, Boston: Butterworth-Heinemann.

Christensen, C. M. & Raynor, M. (2003). *The innovator's solution*, Boston: Harvard Business School Books.

Fox, J. (2000). *How to become a rainmaker: The rules for getting and keeping clients and clients*. New York: Hyperion Books.

McKenna, R. (1993). *Relationship marketing*. New York: Addison-Wesley Publishing.

# APPENDIX A

# Client Service Tools and Recommendations

## Client Service Quick Survey

*Please answer the following in reference to your experience and perceptions.*

1. How do you ensure your client gets the right information? _____
   _____

2. How do you respond to clients' complaints? _____
   _____

3. How do you follow up with clients? _____
   _____

4. Why would a client want to use your service again?_____
   _____

5. How important is Client Relationship Management and why? __
   _____

6. What are the main features of your client service plan? _____
   _____

7. How are you going to monitor your client service plan?_____
   _____

## Client Service Measure: Self

*Circle NT if not true; T if sometimes true; VT if very true. Total your score. The higher the score, the greater your competency in this area.*

| Statements | NT | T | VT |
|---|---|---|---|
| 1.  I always meet clients with a smile. | 1 | 2 | 3 |
| 2.  I know the importance of good listening skills and practice them. | 1 | 2 | 3 |
| 3.  I frequently ask clients if they need additional services. | 1 | 2 | 3 |
| 4.  I constantly self-assess and work to stay current and improve. | 1 | 2 | 3 |
| 5.  I am clear about my role in client service. | 1 | 2 | 3 |
| 6.  I strive to add value to the client and do not accept less from others. | 1 | 2 | 3 |
| 7.  I have a no tolerance policy for unethical behavior with clients. | 1 | 2 | 3 |
| 8.  I keep my e-mails and phone calls to clients clear, concise, and on point. | 1 | 2 | 3 |
| TOTALS | | | |

*This is only an awareness activity to help you form some questions and define some areas of need.*

# 60-Second Introduction Worksheet

*You have only one opportunity to make a good first impression. Maintaining a current and excellent one-minute introduction to yourself is crucial to your success. The worksheet below is designed to help ensure that you have all the bases covered and are prepared to meet new clients.*

| | |
|---|---|
| Hook (10 seconds) | 1. _____<br>2. _____<br>3. _____ |
| Personal Expertise (10 seconds) | 1. _____<br>2. _____<br>3. _____<br>4. _____<br>5. _____ |
| Organization's Strengths (15 seconds) | 1. _____<br>2. _____<br>3. _____ |
| Recent Successes (20 seconds) | 1. _____<br>2. _____<br>3. _____ |
| Information for Follow-Up (10 seconds) | 1. _____<br>2. _____<br>3. _____ |

# Support Client Needs

- Standard communication protocols help ensure that all employees get the same message.

- The three basic elements of any effective conversation: B-M-E

  ◊ **B**eginning—Reveal the facts and clarify the client's needs.

  ◊ **M**iddle—Reach agreement on the common goal and how to achieve it.

  ◊ **E**nd—Keep all promises and follow-up to ensure that needs have been met.

- To reduce miscommunication when a client expresses a concern:

  ◊ Assess whether the client is receptive by paying attention to body language, tone and volume of voice, and facial expressions.

  ◊ Self-monitor to ensure that you are composed and your response promotes dialogue.

  ◊ Identify the milestones in the conversation and apply best practices.

- Rapport-building techniques help in developing positive, long-term relationships. Observe the client and then *subtly*:

  ◊ *Adopt Their Pace*—Speed indicates how information is processed: visually (very fast), auditorially (fast), or kinesthetically (not as fast). Note the client's pattern of movement and match it.

  ◊ *Mirror Their Movements*—Physical mimicry causes the other person to see "someone just like me." Copying posture, facial expressions, eye blinking, hand gestures, and movements, imprints a person with a positive response.

  ◊ *Conform Vocally*—Match the tone, tempo, timbre (quality), and volume of the voice. Also, use the client's favourite words or phrases when responding.

  ◊ *Duplicate Their Chunk Size—Avoid either overwhelming or boring a client by using the level of detail they prefer. For example, if a person tends to give a lot of information at one time, respond with a lot of details. Ask short questions of people who speak in small chunks.*

# The Client Problem Solver

*The B-M-E process below is designed to help you maintain focus so that client concerns are addressed successfully. Use the checklist on the right to determine whether Best Practices are followed.*

## Build Understanding:

1. *Listen. Hear. Understand* what the client wants.

2. Then ask questions to confirm that you have gathered all the facts.

3. Avoid being defensive or making excuses, especially if the client is upset.

☐ Are my emotions under control?

☐ Have I heard everything that the client said from start to finish?

☐ Am I being defensive or making excuses?

☐ Am I staying on point?

☐ Have I asked enough questions to be clear about what the client wants and needs?

☐ What else can I do to engage the client?

_____

_____

## Map a Plan:

1. Work with the client to find the best solution for his or her needs.

2. Take responsibility for what you can control.

   ◊ Determine who can make the decision to move forward.

   ◊ If it is inappropriate for you to act, get the right person immediately.

3. Write down your agreement with the client *while you are talking together* so that no details are lost or misunderstood.

☐ Have I paid diligent attention to all details?

☐ Is the client satisfied with my recommendation?

☐ Is the decision maker involved in the plan?

☐ Am I sure that all promises can be kept?

☐ Have I reviewed the entire plan with the client and gotten agreement on all points?

☐ Have I researched all potential solutions?

☐ What else can I do to help?

_____

_____

## The Client Problem Solver (cont'd)

*The B-M-E process below is designed to help you maintain focus so that client concerns are addressed successfully. Use the checklist on the right to determine whether Best Practices are followed.*

### Ensure Needs Are Met:

1. Do everything you said you would do.
   - ◊ Don't leave any part of the plan unfinished.
   - ◊ Contact the client *before* a deadline is missed to negotiate a new one.
2. Contact the client *before* you make any change in the plan. Don't assume it's okay!
3. Follow-up and make sure that the client is happy with the results.

☐ Have I reviewed the details I wrote down to make sure everything is done?

☐ Have I or my counterparts been completely accessible during the entire process?

☐ Have I kept all of my promises?

☐ Have I followed-up in a timely manner?

☐ What else can I offer to this client?

_____

_____

# CRM 25 Questions

These are great questions to pose at team meetings. Pick one or two per meeting, to keep CRM top of mind.

## What?

1. What do you do when a client complains?
2. What are some of the best things you can do to engage a client in a positive way?
3. What is the best way to win over a client?
4. What is the difference between listening and hearing your client?
5. What are your 3 core values when it comes to CRM?
6. What do you do that is great CRM?
7. What is more important to CRM, handing the client with care or solving their problem?
8. What are the biggest challenges to great CRM?
9. What 2 things could management do to reinforce the importance of CRM?
10. What does CRM mean to you?
11. What things do others do for you that you think is good CRM when you are the client?
12. What can you do to improve client service at an organizational level?
13. What does a client responsive culture look like?
14. What things can you do that will inspire a client to come back?
15. What things are you able to make a decision on when it relates to client service?
16. What things would you like to hear about you as it pertains to client service on a performance evaluation?
17. What are management's expectations as it relates to CRM?
18. What do you use to measure client feedback and satisfaction?
19. What would you like more training on to improve your client service?

20. What is the value of being concise in your communications with clients?
21. What have you done that is over the top for a client?
22. What inspires you to provide great CRM?
23. What is more important, a new client or a returning client?
24. What will you do to be the best at client service?
25. What is the best part about your job as it relates to client service?

## Where?

1. Where does your job as a caretaker of the client begin and end?
2. Where should you refer a problem you can't seem to solve to the client's satisfaction?
3. Where have you experienced excellent client service?
4. Where can you receive guidance on how we do CRM in our organization?
5. Where have you wished you could have been videotaped because you gave such fantastic client service?
6. Where do some clients share their stories of great or bad CRM?
7. Where do we need to sharpen our saw for CRM?
8. Where are we the best at providing client service?
9. Where do you go when you have a positive or negative interaction with a client?
10. Where do you see our organization having a client responsive culture?
11. Where does hiring strategies become an influence over CRM?
12. Where should employees be evaluated on their client service skills?
13. Where do you need to develop your strengths in CRM?
14. Where have you been blown away by the service you received?
15. Where would you like to do some training for CRM because their staff are chronic providers of bad service?
16. Where in the world have you travelled and experienced a culture of client service?
17. Where do you find client service in sport?

18. Where is the best client service at a local restaurant?
19. Where is the best place to communicate with clients?
20. Where do happy clients go?
21. Where is it appropriate to ask for clarification of a client's issue?
22. Where do we need to tweak our CRM model?
23. Where should we log our ideas to improve our CRM?
24. Where do we need to add some energy in our client service to improve our results?
25. Where have you shopped where a salesperson has earned your trust through quality service?

## When?

1. When have you encountered inefficiency in the way we deal with our clients?
2. When you are on the phone with a client how can you win them over?
3. When is it important to evaluate the CRM experience?
4. When you are performing good phone etiquette what things are you doing?
5. When you are performing good face to face CRM what things are you doing?
6. When is it important to see the world through your client's eyes? How do you do that?
7. When you look at your credentials what skills or abilities are missing to ensure that you give great client service?
8. When you look at your credentials what traits and behaviours do you have that make you a great client service resource?
9. When you are setting up an action plan for your client what things do you need to consider?
10. When have you been surprised by a client?
11. When have you been blindsided by a client's level of satisfaction?
12. When have you surprised yourself in a client service interaction?
13. When does CRM influence sales?

14. When have you been rewarded for great CRM?
15. When is flexibility important in client service?
16. When is it OK not to stick to the timeframe you promised to your client?
17. When is it OK not to communicate with a client?
18. When is the time you have made a real difference for a client?
19. When have you gone that extra mile for a client?
20. When have you added more value to a client without adding more paperwork for yourself?
21. When should you be accessible to your clients?
22. When have you been over the top impressed with how a client treated you?
23. When have you felt the support of management in your client service?
24. When do you feel you provide your best service to clients?
25. When is client service worth it?

## Who?

1. Who benefits by engaging in a heated discussion with a client?
2. Who needs to find out about CRM inefficiencies?
3. Whose responsibility is it to ensure that the client is pleased with their service?
4. Who sets the tone for conversations with clients?
5. Who can you go to, to learn new techniques for great client service?
6. Who has given you a great piece of advice for CRM? And what was it?
7. Who do you speak to if you have a concern with a policy that affects CRM in your organization? Can you think of any now?
8. Who at this table have you seen give great client service while at work?
9. Who is a client?
10. Who have you seen demonstrate great body language with clients? What did they do?

11. Who is better at CRM a dog or a cat?  And why?
12. Who should be coaching CRM skills to staff?
13. Who's personality is better for CRM – Martha Stewart or Donald Trump?
14. Who is a great communicator with clients?
15. Who are the clients that make doing client service worthwhile?
16. Who is responsible for communicating the possible solutions?
17. Who has really made your job easier?
18. Who will keep clients in tuff times because of their top notch service?
19. Who in your past is really good with people relationships?
20. Who in government is the best at client service?
21. Who in business is the best at client service?
22. Who on TV demonstrates behaviours that are conducive to great client service?
23. Who sets the vision for CRM?
24. Who are the best types of clients?
25. Who, outside of your industry, should you benchmark your client service after?

## Why?

1. Why is making excuses a bad CRM policy?
2. Why is implementing a client satisfaction survey such an important part of CRM?
3. Why is it important to spend the time to understand the clients question at the beginning of your experience?
4. Why does CRM drive client loyalty to the organization?
5. Why are SLA's and important part of good CRM?
6. Why is ensuring that you understand your clients needs and wants so important?
7. Why is having up to date knowledge about your hard skills so important for client service?

8. Why does what you do in the first 15 seconds of a client experience yield 15 years of loyalty?

9. Why is a how a client feels so important?

10. Why does CRM need to be a culture in the workplace?

11. Why does CRM make you job easier?

12. Why is it important for a employees to have freedom to make decisions?

13. Why are our professional skills so important for client service?

14. Why do people say you are great at client service?

15. Why do you want to provide great service?

16. Why is CRM central to our business activities?

17. Why do we care what people say to others about our client service?

18. Why are we the best at client service in our industry?

19. Why do people want our help?

20. Why do we need to measure regularly our effectiveness in client service?

21. Why are we so good at CRM?

22. Why does leadership philosophy affect client service?

23. Why is it important that CRM is part of the corporate culture?

24. Why is simple etiquette often the best policy for client service?

25. Why is CRM defined by our culture?

# If?

1. If you have to get back to a client about an issue they are experiencing what are some things you should ensure you have before you leave that initial interaction?

2. If a client is confrontational, rude or accusatory what can you do?

3. If you could make one adjustment to the organization to improve CRM what would it be?

4. If you could learn one thing that would help you become better at CRM what would it be?

5. If you owned a company what would be the one thing every employee would do to provide great client service?

6. If you could have a better car or a better car service center which would you choose?

7. If you could stop one pet peeve in client service worldwide what would it be?

8. If you come up with a solution for a client that they can't implement what should you do?

9. If you could sum up your approach to client service in one word what would it be?

10. If something is about to go really wrong with a clients problem what should you do?

11. If there was a master's level university course in CRM what famous person should teach it?

12. If animals ruled the world, what animal would be the best at client service and why?

13. If you have a problem with a product or service, how do you approach the client service agent?

14. If you could suggest one way we could improve our CRM what would you suggest?

15. If management decided to reward great client service, how should they do it?

16. If you see a co-worker providing poor levels of service what would you do?

17. If we could clone one great behaviour or trait for client service into our employees what would it be?

18. If our organization showed that it really supported CRM what would they be doing?

19. If we asked only one question to our clients after our CRM experience what would that question be?

20. If a story book character could teach CRM who would be best served to do so?

21. If we gave an award for the best CRM in our organization who would win?

22. If you could choose just one thing to do more often to give great client service what would that one thing be?

23. If we get an upset client what should we do?

24. If someone having a bad day had to be front line client service personnel what should they focus on?

25. If you had one piece of wisdom about CRM to impart on a new staff member what would that be?

# APPENDIX B

# About TalOp and Other Resources

# TalOp   What is TalOp?

TalOp is the methodology developed by Dr. William Howatt that provides organizations with a model to:

- prevent, predict, and solve problems
- make well-informed decisions
- determine gaps in people and operational processes
- design and develop action plans
- implement initiatives to obtain desired results

Through his years of consulting experience and studies, Dr. Howatt repeatedly observed that most organizations have a disconnect between their strategic vision and results. While most organizations try to either fix their strategic vision or provide support to their leadership, the other aspects of their organizational design are not considered. He realized that his success stories usually turned on the attention to five key aspects of an organization, and that managers and decision-makers needed a means of seeing and analyzing the organization through these five lenses if they wanted to make real and lasting change.

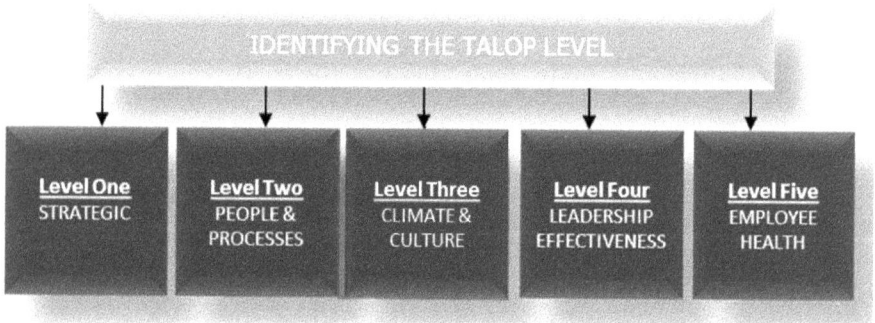

IDENTIFYING THE TALOP LEVEL

| Level One | Level Two | Level Three | Level Four | Level Five |
|---|---|---|---|---|
| STRATEGIC | PEOPLE & PROCESSES | CLIMATE & CULTURE | LEADERSHIP EFFECTIVENESS | EMPLOYEE HEALTH |

TalOp is about aligning talent and operations whenever one of these five lenses is applied. It is a fact-finding approach for improving:

- people effectiveness and engagement
- process efficiency

The ultimate objective is to improve client satisfaction by using accountability and transparency tools. These tools define opportunities, gaps, and risks, and provide a framework for recognizing and solving problems. Using key performance indicators and balance scorecards to monitor and measure results of functions identified (mapping) to maximize efficiency, effectiveness, and engagement, TalOp frames what is needed to improve and maintain an organization's desired level of performance.

# TalOp      Function Mapping

Function Mapping is a TalOp tool for gathering data that is important to a management team for understanding and monitoring the functions of an organization. By developing a scorecard that applies across an entire department or organization, function mapping offers both a dashboard and a deeper dive into the functioning of an organization. Function mapping provides transparency as to what functions are being done and who is accountable for each.

### What is a function map?

Function mapping is an operations management tool for improving consistency, accountability, communications, and quality across an organization:

- It is a tool for facilitating operational decision making.
- The function map is dynamic and will change with the organization.

Seen from a distance, a function map might look like a colourful organizational chart — but don't be fooled. The TalOp function map is not an organization chart. Instead, it focuses on *outputs*, not positions. It reports all the functions (outputs or deliverables) being done, or performed. The report includes data describing the purpose and nature of each function, where it resides in the organization, and the current state of its people effectiveness, efficiency, output capacity, knowledge management, and safety practices. This data can be communicated in a series of paper reports or via a visual graphic that captures all functions, grouped by domain.

### What is a function?

A function is a logical grouping of two or more tasks that create an output (a product or service).

### What type of data do you gather about each function?

As part of the TalOp suite of tools, TalOp function mapping gathers data not only on the outputs (the number of products, the quality standards of the products or services but also data on the capacity and capability of the talent and people who perform the functions and the operational processes required to perform them. By gathering data on key attributes of all functions, the function mapping process gives managers an opportunity to understand the impact of systemic concerns or issues across a group of functions or across an entire organization. This information provides data for evidence-based decision-making from the frontline right up to the CEO.

Visit www.TalOp.com to learn more about TalOp function mapping and how it can support improved management practices in your organization.

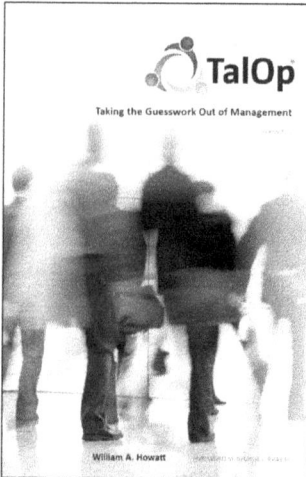

TalOp is a strategy for aligning **Talent** (People) and **Operations** (Processes). TalOp is a disciplined, fact-finding approach for improving *People Effectiveness and Engagement* and *Process Efficiency*. TalOp's objective is to improve client satisfaction through enhancing organization-wide accountability and transparency.

TalOp assists organizations/divisions/groups to define opportunities, gaps, and risks. It provides a framework for defining and solving problems and setting priorities through a fact-based decision process.

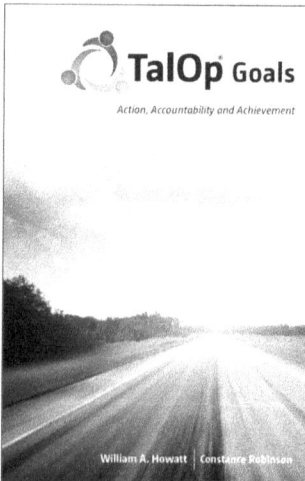

*TalOp Goals* addresses the three fundamental areas for success: goals for the quality organization, goals for work performance, and goals for life performance. Each type of goals needs tending to ensure success, and each is addressed in this latest TalOp publication. Learn the step-by-step approach for developing strategic plans and building action plans that reach all levels of the organization. Explore tools for developing meaningful performance goals that are directly tied to strategic outcomes. Recognize the need for personal development opportunities that sustain your top performers and grow your talent.

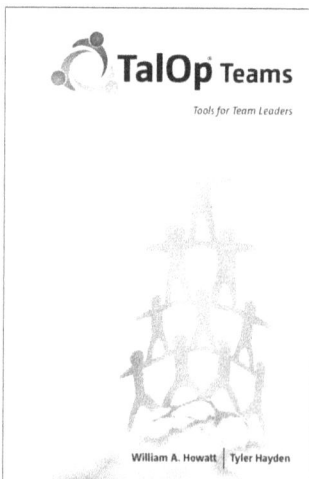

In response to the need for a set of tools to address the ever-changing landscape of business, thought leaders Dr. Bill Howatt and Tyler Hayden take us to a new level of leading teams. *TalOp Teams — Tools for Team Leaders* offers a comprehensive and easy-to-use set of principles and tools that will help managers and leaders better understand the groups they lead.

Each chapter provides leaders with standalone strategies for understanding team make-up or insights on what leaders can do to influence their teams' behaviours and results.

## 2 Elements for Employee and Labour Relations

This book assists HR professionals and managers to appreciate the complexity of employee relations and how critical it is to understand how to facilitate and implement effective employee relations strategies. Having defined policies and procedures is only a piece of the equation; understanding how to facilitate and implement them in a collaborative and respectful manner is most imperative.

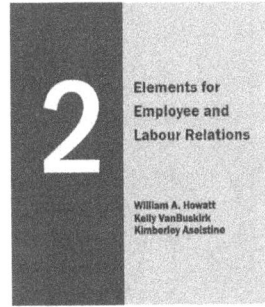

## Mediation and Negotiation

Mediation and negotiation are core skills that help managers avoid disagreements in the workplace. Both skills have an application for helping parties formulate agreement; however, there are times when a manager will be best served by using mediation skills and others when it makes more sense to negotiate a position. This program introduces these two skills and helps managers apply them in their daily roles.

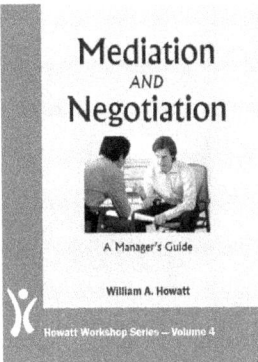

## Coaching 101 for Managers

One of the most effective ways to develop a skilled workforce is to develop people skills and capacity from within the organization. One of the best power skills a manager can have is coaching. The ability to effectively communicate with others is a necessary expectation before one will be able to coach. The purpose of *Coaching 101 for Managers* is to provide managers with a path and framework for adapting coaching to their leadership approach, both formally and informally.

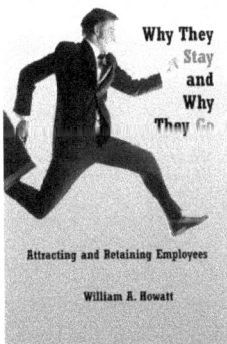

## Why They Stay and Why They Go

The single biggest competitive advantage any organization can have today is its people. Research has proven that attracting the right talent and reducing turnover have a direct financial benefit. This book examines some of the reasons why employees come to an organization and why they stay. An organization that creates a supportive culture and effective management that facilitates employee engagement and job satisfaction is on the way to becoming an employer of choice.

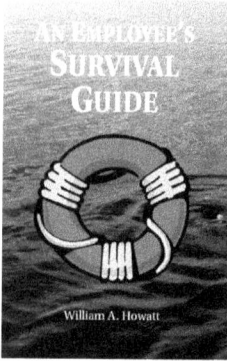

## An Employee's Survival Guide

This book explores some of the basic knowledge and skills that too often are assumed employees have fully developed when they come to work. We all may have different needs and core values, but there are some fundamental skills that you will be well served to focus on throughout your career, regardless of your role. This book helps you to continue developing and improving those basic skills.

## Engage Your Workforce

For an organization to successfully climb to the summit of success (productivity and profitability) it must have a clear vision and plan. There are no shortcuts and the organization's ultimate success will require an engaged workforce. This book focuses on leadership skills for assertiveness, difficult conversations, and conflict resolution.

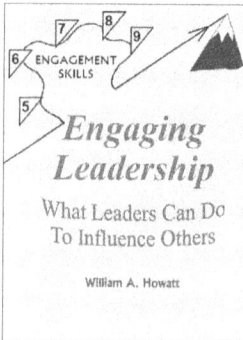

## Engaging Leadership

For an organization to successfully climb to the summit of success (productivity and profitability) it must have a clear vision and plan. There are no shortcuts and the organization's ultimate success will require an engaged workforce. This book focuses on leadership skills for communicating with and influencing others.

## Engage Your Clients

For an organization to successfully climb to the summit of success (productivity and profitability) it must have a clear vision and plan. There are no shortcuts and the organization's ultimate success will require an engaged workforce. This book focuses on leadership skills for thinking and selling their point of view.

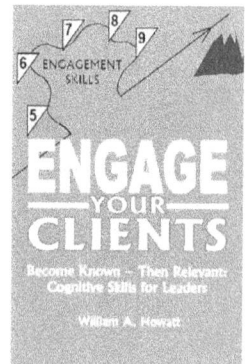

# Meet the authors . . .

## William A. Howatt
PhD, EdD, Post Doc Behavioural Science
UCLA School of Medicine

is recognized as an international strategic HR expert who works with organizations throughout the world to develop their most valuable resource — their human capital. Through his commitment to excellence, passion for learning, and teaching with a dash of humour he works with organizations and teams to achieve results in their quest to manage and develop their talent.

## Tyler Hayden

Author, thought-leader and hilarious keynoter is the founder of the *Message In a Bottle Book* series, international leadership and team consultant, and elected government official. He has over two decades of experience as a speaker and organizational consultant, and is the author of over a dozen books and measures on leadership and team building.

Tyler regularly scores as the top keynote speaker at conferences and meetings.

## Constance Robinson
BA, MA, LLB

A labour and employment lawyer, and a certified human resource professional (CHRP), Constance works with management teams to solve the people challenges in organizations.

In addition to working with private sector clients, Constance provides research and advice to public policymakers with respect to workplace and constitutional issues in education, health, and the public service.